THE HORSE LIBRARY

WESTERN RIDING

MARY HUGHES

CHELSEA HOUSE PUBLISHERS

PHILADELPHIA

Frontis: Team ropers work together to bring down a steer at a rodeo in Rosebud, South Dakota.

CHELSEA HOUSE PUBLISHERS

EDITOR IN CHIEF Sally Cheney
ASSOCIATE EDITOR IN CHIEF Kim Shinners
PRODUCTION MANAGER Pamela Loos
ART DIRECTOR Sara Davis

STAFF FOR *WESTERN RIDING*

EDITOR Sally Cheney
ASSOCIATE ART DIRECTOR Takeshi Takahashi
SERIES DESIGNER Keith Trego

CHESTNUT PRODUCTIONS AND CHOPTANK SYNDICATE, INC.

EDITORIAL AND PICTURE RESEARCH Mary Hull and Norman Macht
LAYOUT AND PRODUCTION Lisa Hochstein

http://www.chelseahouse.com

First Printing

1 3 5 7 9 8 6 4 2

Library of Congress Cataloguing-in-Publication Data Applied For.

Horse Library SET: 0-7910-6650-9
Western Riding: 0-7910-6655-X

TABLE OF CONTENTS

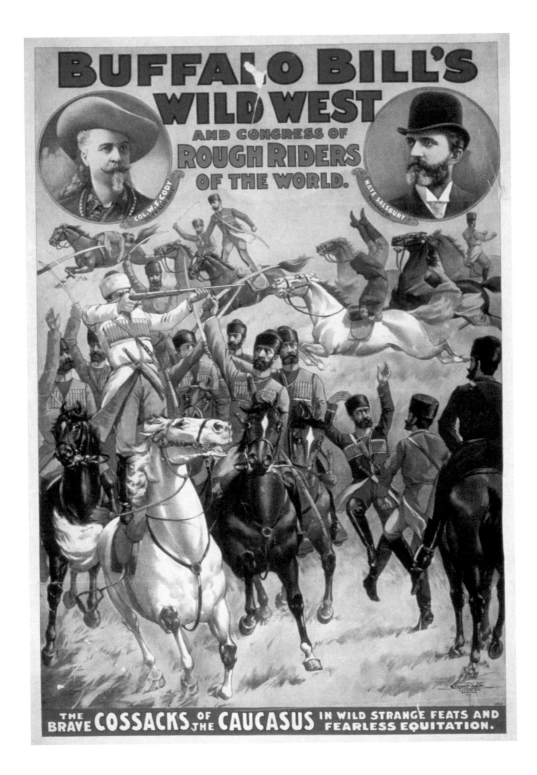

An 1899 poster for Buffalo
Bill Cody's Wild West show
promises spectators plenty
of excitement, including
live western animals and
the daring exploits of
"Cossacks" on horseback.

THE PONY EXPRESS

The opening of the American West in the 1840s and '50s uprooted thousands of families, who packed wagons and headed west for a new life. Prized possessions, kindly neighbors, friendly townsfolk, and cherished loved ones were left behind. Once the new frontier had been reached, a different problem arose. With so much territory between East and West, how would westerners ever manage to keep abreast of what was happening back East? Anyone entrusted to carry a message faced a treacherous trip across 3,000 miles.

Telegraph lines fell woefully short of completely crossing the newly expanded nation. The task of laying railroad ties from one end of the country to the other was well under way, but far from finished. Ships sailed from the East to the West coast, but they had to sail all the way around South America to reach California. The journey was long and extremely time consuming.

For a long time, no one seemed overly concerned about the length of time it took for news to cross the continent. Everyone was resigned to the fact that mail might take months to reach its intended recipients. Gradually, however, businessmen took it upon themselves to try to remedy the situation.

Stagecoach men knew all about the dangers that cross-country travel could bring. They operated their stagecoach lines through miles of western territory and were often asked to transport mail along with passengers. Coaches were cumbersome, and made for slow going up long, winding mountainsides. These stagecoach men believed that eliminating the stagecoaches would speed up the delivery of the mail. What they needed were not slow coaches, but fast horses with light riders who wouldn't weigh them down.

Naturally, a horse would need rest, as would a rider; but what if a relay system were set up with the rider switching his sack of mail to a fresh horse after so many miles? Then, when the rider tired, he could hand off his mail sack to a rested rider all set to mount yet another fresh horse and take off. That would save precious time. It would cost more to hire extra riders and purchase extra horses, but people might be willing to pay a little more to have their mail arrive that much more quickly.

Charles H. Russell of the Central Overland Stage Company thought the idea of a relay system had promise. He established the Pony Express, with runs between St. Joseph, Missouri, and Sacramento, California. Ships carried the mail between Sacramento and San Francisco. Russell bought six hundred horses that were fast, yet tough enough to endure the often perilous trail conditions. To ride the horses, Russell and his partner, Alexander Majors, interviewed hundreds of boys and young men eager to land this exciting new job.

Russell and Majors were looking for riders who weighed under 110 pounds. But they were also looking for brave young souls who had a good sense of horsemanship and could shoot well. Pony Express riders were apt to come under Indian attack in their travels, and Russell made it clear that he wanted the mail to get through. Patrons were going to be paying $5 a letter for Pony Express service, and he did not want them disappointed.

In the end, seventy-five "Pony Boys" were hired to ride for the Pony Express. They earned $100 to $150 a month—equivalent to about $2,000–$3,000 today. They were issued uniforms consisting of red shirts, blue trousers, fringed buckskin jackets, and boots with silver spurs. They were then entrusted with a mochila, which held the mail to be delivered. A mochila was a large leather square designed to be positioned over a saddle. One opening fit nicely over the rear of the saddle where it rose to the high, rounded rim called the "cantle," while another hole allowed the Pony Boy to slide the mochila down over the saddle horn. There were padlocked leather boxes for the mail at each of the four corners of the mochila. Swapping a mochila from one mount to another could be done quickly and easily, helping to expedite the delivery of the mail.

Mr. Russell was entrusting a lot to his Pony Boys, but he was also expecting a lot from the spirited horses he had bought. He knew it wouldn't take long for the horses to learn their routes, traveling each day to a relay station and then back again on the return trip. There was a reason Russell instructed his riders to fasten the leather mochila holding the mail onto their horses and not themselves. Should a rider be shot and fall from the saddle, the horse—still carrying the mail—would more than likely continue on to the relay station.

Every day except Sunday, one Pony Boy would leave from the Missouri starting point at noon, heading west. Coming from the other direction, one Pony Boy would also leave Sacramento at 8:00 a.m. each day. Each Pony Boy was given six hours to cover a distance of about sixty miles. Along the way he would change horses, using six different ponies during his stretch of the mail run. At the end of his run, the rider would hand off his mochila to the next rider, who would cover approximately sixty more miles. In ten days, the mail from one end of the Pony Express route would reach the other. It was a vast improvement over the slow and unreliable mail delivery of the past.

 The First Pony Express Ride

The west-bound mail to be carried cross-country via the first Pony Express ride was transported by train until it reached St. Joseph, Missouri. An excited crowd gathered to witness the start of the new service. Unfortunately, some spectators wanted souvenirs as well. So many people began plucking hairs from a frightened Pony Express mare's mane and tail that Mr. Majors finally sent the pony and its rider back to the stable to await the train away from the crowd. Years later, rings and watch chains, supposedly braided from the hair of the first pony to ride for the Pony Express, surfaced for sale.

A Pony Express rider flees from unfriendly Indians in this 1860s litho-graph. Pony Express riders were heavily armed and their mail pouches were tied to their saddles to ensure that, if something happened to them, their horses could still deliver the mail to the next station.

The Pony Express kicked off its first run in St. Joseph, Missouri, on April 3, 1860. Henry Wallace was given the honor of being the first rider heading west. His mochila held a copy of a telegraphed message from President Buchanan in Washington. There was a lot of pomp and ceremony heralding the beginning of the new mail service. The town of St. Joseph turned out for the send off.

For two years, the Pony Express was very popular with merchants and bankers. Armed Pony Express riders rode day and night, in all kinds of weather. Only once did they lose any mail. But, in 1862, the telegraph wires that connected the country's East Coast to St. Joseph, Missouri, finally reached the West Coast. The railroad followed. There was no longer a need for the Pony Express.

One of the Pony Boys, William F. Cody, managed to carve out a niche for himself in the pages of American history. After his stint as a Pony Boy, Cody became a scout for the U.S. Army, and after that tried his hand at buffalo hunting. He soon earned the nickname of Buffalo Bill Cody. Because so many hunters were hard at work trying to eke out an existence in the depressed economy following the Civil War, millions of buffalo were slaughtered for their hides. Herds were wiped out, endangering not only the buffalo species, but also the lives of the Native Americans who had depended on the buffalo for their way of life.

With the buffalo herds on the wane, the ways of the West were changing. Buffalo Bill Cody recognized this, and put together a traveling show so that those who had not witnessed the West first hand could experience the thrills of the Wild West as a spectator. The show toured the United States and, at the urging of author Mark Twain, even went abroad in 1887. In England, thirty to forty thousand people a day came to watch America's West come to life.

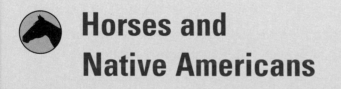

Horses and Native Americans

Horses changed the Native American's way of life drastically. Before the Spanish reintroduced the horse to North America in the 16th century, Native Americans subsisted on food they tracked and hunted on foot. Typically, Native Americans exhausted the supply of game in an area before moving on. Strapping their belongings to themselves and to their dogs, they could only progress as far as they could travel on foot.

In 1876 the discovery of gold in the black hills of South Dakota created the town of Deadwood, a rough mining town that was home to "Wild" Bill Hickok and Calamity Jane. The stagecoach was the primary means of transportation until the railroad reached Deadwood in 1891, spelling the end of the stagecoach era. This 1890 photograph shows the last of the Deadwood coaches.

Buffalo Bill Cody's Wild West Show was a huge success, largely because audiences weren't seeing actors. They were seeing real live elk, donkeys, deer, longhorn Texas steers, and over a dozen buffalo. They were watching genuine cowboys and Native Americans riding 181 Western horses.

The Pony Express is gone. There is now but a single herd of twenty wild buffalo roaming within the boundaries of Yellowstone National Park. But the Western horse, far from disappearing, has remained a mainstay over the course of time.

Appaloosas are synonymous with the Wild West; they take their name from "the Palouse," a region of the American Northwest that was once populated by Nez Perce Indians, who selectively bred the horses to be fast, strong, and sure footed.

WESTERN STYLE

The easiest way to tell English riders from Western riders is to look at their clothing. Western riders favor tall, wide-brimmed cowboy hats and high-heeled cowboy boots. Sometimes just for show, and sometimes to coax a horse to move more quickly, a Western rider will strap on a pair of spurs. Spurs attach to the rider's boots. Each spur has a metal wheel of spikes with which the rider can dig into the horse's side to "spur" it on to quicken its pace. When not riding his horse, a cowboy wearing spurs has a no-nonsense jingle-jangle to his walk. The unmistakable sound of his spurs makes his presence known as soon as he strides into a room.

15

Western riders often wear protective leather chaps over their jeans or frontier pants. Chaps are the leather leggings traditionally worn by Western ranch hands. Shot-gun chaps are somewhat narrow, buckled around the waist, and zipped up on each leg. Bat-wing chaps are clipped together at the sides of the legs.

An English rider wears a rounded, small-brimmed riding hat which is quite different from the typical wide-brimmed cowboy hat that shades the rider's eyes and face from the sun. The English riding hat is a hard hat intended to afford some protection to the rider's head. It is meant to be worn with the chin strap securely fastened. The boots worn by an English rider are ankle high, unless the rider is a jumper, in which case the boots are knee high. Classic English riding pants are light colored breeches, or jodphurs. These form-fitting pants give a much smoother and streamlined appearance than the riveted, denim jeans of the Western rider. For shows and competitions English riders may wear formal riding jackets or top coats over their riding attire, giving a polished look to the entire ensemble. They may also wear a dress hat known as a top hat, or derby.

Like their riders, the English and Western horses themselves are outfitted differently. The Western saddle features a high pommel, or horn. A ranch hand or rodeo competitor may keep his lariat close at hand, hanging from the saddle's pommel. The Western saddle itself is apt to be "tooled" with elaborate designs hand-carved into the leather with a small, pointed tool called an awl. The rear of the saddle rises to a high, rounded rim called the cantle, which prevents the rider from sliding too far back on his horse.

The long, leather stirrups hang low so that the rider's legs can be almost fully extended with very little bend at the knee. The stirrups are also large enough to accommodate

Riding attire for Western horse shows includes wide-brimmed cowboy hats and riding chaps, which are usually made from leather or suede.

the cowboy boots of the Western horseman. The combination of the steady Western saddle and stirrups make it relatively easy for a rider to maintain his balance atop a horse, compared to riding the same horse bareback.

In contrast, the smooth English saddle has a very low cantle and pommel. Stirrups are made of metal, and the stirrup length is shorter, to accommodate the English riding style of leaning forward, keeping the knees bent. Beneath the saddle, helping to cushion the horse and prevent saddle sores, an English rider places a saddle pad, while the Western rider positions a saddle blanket there for the same purpose.

The way a horse moves is called its "gait." A slow, even gait is a walk. When a horse is walking, it moves just one foot at a time. It is said that a walk has four beats, one beat for each hoof hitting the ground. A horse's walk may be fast, but it must not bounce the rider up and down.

Sometimes the same movement is called different names. For instance, English riders refer to the bouncy gait that falls between a walk and a canter in speed as a trot, while Western riders sometimes label that same gait a jog. This gait is said to have two beats, because two of the horse's hooves hit the ground at the same time. For example, the hooves of a horse's right hind leg and left front leg

 # Horses and the Conquistadors

In 1598 Spanish conquerer, or conquistador, Juan de Onate took over the farmlands of the Pueblo Indians of northern Mexico. The soldiers and settlers who accompanied him brought sheep, cattle, and horses. The Pueblo people were reduced to being servants and slaves for the Spanish and were forbidden to ride horses. Other tribes of the plains quickly realized the value of the four-legged imports and frequent raids on the Spanish corrals resulted.

would hit the ground together, counting as the first beat, alternating with the hooves of its left hind leg and right front leg touching down for the second beat.

A gait with long, swinging steps is called a canter in English riding circles. That same gait is known as a lope to Western riders. There are three beats to a lope. If the left hind hoof touches down first for the first beat, it will be followed by the right hind and left front hooves hitting the ground simultaneously for the second beat. The third beat is marked by the right front hoof touching down, just before all four hooves are suspended momentarily in the air.

Galloping is the fastest of all gaits. It requires the horse to take long strides. Like the walk, the gallop consists of four beats, because each hoof touches the ground independently. However, because the gallop is much faster than the walk, and because a galloping horse actually pushes off with a front hoof, the horse again becomes suspended above the ground briefly, as it does during the lope.

To further distinguish the speed of a horse at any given time, each gait is said to have three different speeds. Any gait might be performed at a slow, regular, or fast speed. Usually a slow gait is associated with working. When a horse stops moving, it is said to come to a halt.

The Western style of riding grew out of the necessities of managing livestock on a ranch. The reins were always held in one hand, freeing the Western rider's other hand, to perform the day-to-day chores of ranching. In contest situations, a Western rider needs one hand free to compete in such activities such as calf-roping and steer wrestling. Today, with the number of ranches dwindling, and the popularity of Western riding competitions growing, more horses are trained for the contest circuit than for actual stock work.

A western saddle has a high pommel and cantle, which help keep the rider in the seat. Show saddles are often elaborately decorated with silver and tooled leather.

Today's Western riders might compete in any of four different classes, choosing from such divisions as the Western Riding Horse, the Pleasure horse, the Trail Horse, or the Parade Horse.

According to Mary Gordon-Watson's *Handbook of Riding*:

> In the Western Riding and Trail Horse classes, the horses are judged on both their behavior and skills. The Western Riding Horse is required to show his paces, manners, and suitability as an all-around conveyance; the Trail Horse must show his ability to negotiate a variety of obstacles and willingness to carry awkward objects.
>
> In the Western Pleasure Horse division, the judges are looking for a well-turned-out combination of horse and rider which they regard as a perfect example of the well-trained partnership. The

horse is required to perform at different paces according to the judge's preference, and is judged on performance and conformation.

The Parade Horse is required to display himself to music. He will be lavishly 'dressed', since his appearance is of primary importance. Attractive Palominos, Pintos, Appaloosas, Arabs, Morgans and walking horses are usually the most successful in these show classes. The horse will also be judged on conformation, paces, performance and manners.

A Western horse may be one of several different breeds. Each breed has its own distinct characteristics, history, and horse association.

The Appaloosa

The Nez Perce tribe of the Pacific Northwest bred a unique spotted horse and named it the Appaloosa, after the Palouse River. These Native Americans owned the lands in that river's valley and were quite skilled in horse breeding. The Nez Perce wanted a beautiful, reliable workhorse. The Appaloosa was carefully derived from strong, spotted horses of Spanish stock. As a result, the hardy breed is known for its strength and adaptability, in addition to its trademark spotted coat.

Within the Appaloosa breed there are five very different and distinct coat patterns. An Appaloosa may have a blanket, frost, leopard, marble, or snowflake coat pattern.

The blanket-patterned Appaloosa has a blanket of white over its hips. Some blanket Appaloosas may have dark spots on this blanket of white. An Appaloosa is said to have a frost pattern if the horse is primarily dark with a white speckling. A leopard Appaloosa is just the opposite. Its dark spots are sprinkled over a white background. A marble-coated Appaloosa may deviate from the typical red or blue roan horse coloring by having a frost pattern on its midsection, with darker coloring at its head and hindquarters. A snowflake- patterned Appaloosa has lots of spots over its hip area.

Regardless of the pattern on its coat, an Appaloosa will have a short, sparse mane, vertical stripes on its hooves, black and white spotting on its nose, and a white "sclera"— a white outer membrane of the eyeball—around each eye.

In 1877, when the tribal lands of the Nez Perce were seized by United States troops, the Appaloosa—and its breeders—were nearly wiped out. In 1938 the Appaloosa Horse Club of Moscow, Idaho, began to popularize the breed, making sure that this good-tempered horse was not lost to the world.

Pintos and Paints

There was a time when part-colored horses were known simply as calicos, much like the popular breed of cats by that name. In today's specialized world, however, a distinction is made between the Pinto and the Paint horse, even though both types of part-colored horses take their names from the same Spanish word. It's easy to understand how this happened, because pintado is the Spanish word for "painted." Pinto is the shortened, American version of pintado, while Paint is the American translation of the word's meaning.

Today, both the Paint horse and the Pinto horse each have their own horse association. The American Paint Horse Association recognizes horses with registered Paint, Quarter Horse, and Thoroughbred bloodlines. The requirements for the Pinto Horse Association are somewhat less exacting. The organization registers any horse or pony meeting its color requirements. This makes it harder to award breed status to the Pinto, because the broad grouping allows such a wide difference in type and size of animal.

When a Paint or Pinto has an overall solid-colored coat splashed with irregular white markings, it is said to have *ovaro* coloring. If, instead, a horse is predominately white with dark irregular splashes of color, it is described as having *tobiano* coloring. Pintos and Paints with black and white coloring are labeled piebald, while the term skewbald refers to those with any colors besides black and white.

Paints and Pintos are powerful horses that lend themselves to riding. Not surprisingly, these sensible horses were especially popular with cowboys who spent so much of their lives in the saddle.

Palomino

The word palomino has come to mean golden. Accordingly, the horse of that name may range in height, but must be golden in color. The mane and the tail of the Palomino are both silvery white, making the horse strikingly beautiful.

Breeding a Palomino with another Palomino may not produce a palomino-colored horse. For this reason, Palominos are usually bred by crossing a horse that is palomino in color with one that is chestnut, or by breeding a chestnut-colored horse with an albino, or all-white horse. For a Palomino to meet the requisites of the American Palomino Horse Association, one of its parents must be a Quarter Horse, Arabian, or Thoroughbred, while the other parent must be a registered Palomino.

Another descendant from the horses brought to America by the Spanish, the Palomino is comfortable in the hot climate of the west.

Palominos are golden-colored and have white manes and tails.

The Mustang

The English word mustang comes from the Spanish "mestena", which means "group or herd of horses." If any horse meets the romantic equestrian notion of the Wild West, it is the Mustang. Descended from the horses brought to the Americas from Spain in the 16th century, this free-spirited breed developed in the wild. Horses that had strayed or were set free by the cattle ranchers of Mexico formed their own herds that migrated north to run wild in North America's western plains. True to their Spanish bloodlines, they were of hardy stock, very agile, and often quite fast. Free to breed among themselves, their numbers grew to an estimated one million in 1900.

As Americans pushed westward, claiming more and more land for their grazing sheep and cattle, the roaming room for the Mustang diminished drastically. Anxious to protect their grazing land, some farmers and ranchers hunted down Mustangs, flushing them out into the open by using low-flying aircraft. The wild horses were then chased to the point of exhaustion by jeeps and trucks. Tired and hurt, the once proud horses were eventually sent to the slaughter-house to be processed and sold as canned horsemeat.

The fastest and the smartest of the Mustangs managed to avoid these traps set by man, but thousands of less fortunate Mustangs were killed before this inhumane practice was put to an end. President Eisenhower signed a bill on September 8, 1959, making it illegal for hunters to use airplanes and motor vehicles to flush out and run down wild horses. In December of 1962 the United States Department

Hunting On Horseback

Once the Nez Perce Indians learned to ride horses, they were able to track the American bison, or buffalo, across the plains. The tribe valued their horses, and carefully chose which ones to breed. The less desirable horses were traded away. The most valued horses were those the men rode into war. The spotted coat of the Appaloosa was not only beautiful, it also helped to camouflage the horse in battle.

of the Interior established America's first refuge for wild horses. Located in the Nevada desert, the refuge was made up of 435,000 acres of land spotted with springs and watering holes for the wild horses. It was the first of many such parcels of land that would later be set aside to preserve the horses that had run free for so many years in the dwindling American wilderness.

Bands of wild Mustangs were such a symbolic part of America's western frontier that many people believed the wild horses were native to America. The horses that were native to the continent disappeared some 10,000 years ago. No one knows what caused the disappearance of those horses. But the emergence of the Mustangs, running wild through the plains, with nothing to fence them in but the distant, surrounding mountains, seemed to satisfy the nation's desire to have a horse to call its own.

Eventually, too much inbreeding among the herds of horses weakened some of the once-strong lines that had been handed down from the horses first brought over by the Spanish. Still, some of the wild Mustangs of today are fortunate to bear a resemblance to their hardy Spanish ancestors in either appearance or strength. Luxuriant manes and tails, and strong and sturdy legs with hooves that do not require shoes are hallmarks of the American Mustang.

The Quarter Horse

Horses were brought to the colony of Virginia by the British in 1611, and they were later bred with horses of Spanish stock. The resulting horses had massive hindquarters which gave the animals explosive starting speed. The colonists called these horses "Quarter Horses" when they learned that the speed of the breed was excellent for the distance of about one quarter-mile. Owing largely to its remarkable ability to break into a sprint from a standing start, this breed quickly dominated the short races set up by the settlers.

To earn his keep in American history, the Quarter Horse had to do more than race. The healthy horse with its wide hips and sturdy, heavily muscled legs, was counted on to perform a wide range of chores. Early Americans used the horse in their heaviest hauling and farming work. The Quarter Horse was also used to round up cattle.

While the free-range Mustang managed to capture the heart and spirit of the American west, the Quarter Horse is the first true all-American breed and the most popular horse breed worldwide.

In team roping two horses and two riders work together to tie up a steer; the "header" rides ahead and tries to rope the steer's head or horns, while the "heeler" stays behind to rope the animal's hindlegs.

THE RODEO

Running, jumping, bucking, herding, playing, and pulling are considered the six basic talents that horses naturally possess. A horseman must observe which of these talents are most apparent in a particular horse to determine how that horse will be best used.

A horse with any amount of natural speed will usually show its quickness to those with watchful eyes. Horses who like to jump or buck will likely do just that while at play. Those that jump the highest may be well suited to become jumpers, while those that have a definite disdain for riders may wind up as "bucking broncos." The word "bronco" comes from an old

Spanish word meaning something rough. True to their name, broncos are typically rough to handle, making them ideal mounts for saddle bronc competitions.

Cow horses tend to display a natural affinity toward herding. Usually these horses seem to dominate those around them. Instinctively, they herd the other horses together, knowing that there is a comfortable safety in numbers. Cow horses usually excel at roping and cutting contests.

A playful, dancing horse that is happiest when prancing, spinning, turning, and frolicking about will probably lend itself well to reining competitions. For years they were designated to pull plows, wagons, and carriages to earn their keep, but nowadays these horses may wind up in competitions featuring pulling and driving.

Calf Roping

If a rancher wants to administer medicine to a sick calf, he has to first rope and tie down the ailing animal. Calf roping contests in a rodeo setting mimic those motions, except that the calves used in competitions are quite healthy, usually very feisty, and given a head start.

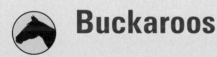

Buckaroos

From the end of the Civil War until the mid 1880's, the cowboy was king. Calling themselves "buckaroos," the American cowboys unwittingly paid tribute to their Mexican counterparts by mispronouncing "vaquero," the Spanish word for cowboy. North or south of the border, cowboys learned to rope and ride, rounding up cattle for landowners who needed their calves branded, and their herds driven to market.

To rope a calf, cowboys must be adept at swinging a rope while on horseback. Their horses need to be well practiced in the art of the sliding stop, for once a calf has been lassoed, the cowboy must jump down from his horse, run to the calf, and tie any three of its legs together, using what's called a pigging string. If the calf has fallen to the ground during the roping, the cowboy must allow the animal to regain its footing, and then bring it to the ground once more. This is called flanking the calf. After successfully tying the calf, the cowboy signals the judges by throwing both of his hands into the air, then mounts his horse and allows his rope to go slack. If the calf does not kick free within the next six seconds, the cowboy has done his job.

Calf roping must be done quickly if a cowboy wants to see his name in rodeo's record books. In 1997 Jeff Chapman of Athens, Texas, performed the task in a record 6.8 seconds at the National Finals Rodeo.

Team Roping

Most rodeo contests involve only a cowboy and his horse. In team roping, there are two horses and two riders working together as a team to bring down a steer. Because the two human team members each have such distinct jobs to perform in the event, titles are awarded separately to the event's winners. The team's "header," who rides ahead and tries to rope the steer by the head or horns, is competing only against other headers in rankings, while the team's "heeler," who stays behind to rope the steer's hind legs, competes only against other heelers.

In team roping, the header comes out of the box first. He and his horse chase down a steer which has been given a head start. The header must then rope the steer in one of the following ways: around the head and one horn; around the neck; or around both horns. To prevent injuries, the horns of the steer are protectively wrapped, for this event. The header must then turn to the left, with the steer following behind him.

Next it is up to the heeler to rope both of the steer's hind legs. Roping just one hind leg will cost the heeler a five-second penalty. Committing a crossfire, or throwing the rope before the header has successfully changed the direction of the steer, is grounds for disqualification.

At the National Finals Rodeo in 1994, a team from Arizona caught 10 steers in 59.1 seconds. Both the header, Jake Barnes, and the heeler, Clay O'Brien Cooper, have been named team roping world champions seven times.

The United States Team Roping Championships were founded in 1990 to promote the sport of Team Roping. Today there are over 37,000 participating members.

Saddle Bronc Riding

A saddle bronc will do its best to throw anyone attempting to ride it, and a rodeo rider must stay aboard a bronco for an eight-second ride. On the ranches of the Old West, cowboys held their own contests to see who could manage to stay atop a horse that had not yet been broken. Today, feisty saddle bronc horses are bred specifically for rodeo.

In the rodeo arena, rules stipulate that riders must begin their rides with their feet over the bronc's shoulders. This gives the horse the advantage, and many would-be riders will be thrown long before the buzzer signals that eight seconds have passed.

The best of the bronc riders manage to coordinate the actions of their own feet with the movements of the bucking horse. Their feet will be to the rear of the saddle as the horse bucks, but will move back toward the neck of the

Saddle bronc riding pits cowboys against horses that are bred to buck; the cowboy must keep his balance and manage to stay on the horse for at least eight seconds.

horse just before the horse touches his front feet to the ground. This is all part of a rider's spurring actions.

A rider that is thrown from the horse prematurely will be disqualified, but a rider may also be disqualified for improper feet positioning at the beginning of the ride; for touching himself, the horse, or his equipment with his free hand; for letting a foot slip out of a stirrup; or for dropping the reins.

Saddle bronc riders are awarded points for how hard the horse bucks, and how much control they exhibit while atop the bronco, as well as for their all-important spurring actions.

The winner of six saddle bronc riding titles, and numerous other rodeo titles and championships, the late, legendary cowboy, Casey Tibbs, is generally acknowledged to have been the best of the bronc riders. The Pro Rodeo Hall of Fame in Colorado Springs, Colorado, proudly displays a 20-foot bronze statue of the South Dakota cowboy outside its doors. Billy Etbauer of Ree Heights, South Dakota, was the event's World Champion for the year 2000.

Bareback Riding

Before the invention of the saddle, mounting and dismounting a horse required a good deal of athletic ability. Staying on a mount also required stamina and a strong sense of balance.

In the rodeo, a bareback rider comes out of the chute with his feet positioned above the break of the horse's shoulder. His feet must remain there until the horse hits the ground on its initial jump. Failing to "mark out" the horse like that will result in the rider being disqualified.

In competition, a bareback ride lasts for eight seconds, during which time the rider may hold on with only one hand to the leather and rawhide bareback rigging. He must not touch himself, the horse, or the rigging, with his other hand.

A Cowboy's Saddle

A cowboy invested a whole month's wages of $35 to $40 in his saddle (an amount equivalent to $700–800 today). It was the most expensive piece of equipment he owned. A good cowboy was never without his saddle. By day, he sat in his saddle, often riding from dawn to dusk. At night a cowboy would rest his weary head on the leather worn smooth from riding, using his saddle as a pillow as he slept under the stars.

The rider spurs the horse on with his feet during the short and often wild ride.

In the world of bareback riding, the standings are often ranked in terms of the riders' earnings for a single year. The mark to beat is held by Marvin Garrett, who earned $136,733 in 1995. Garrett has been the World Champion Bareback Rider four times.

Barrel Racing

Barrel racers are timed as they gallop their horses around a racecourse marked off with barrels. The object is for the

Barrel racers ride at high speed and must make tight turns around barrels without knocking them over.

horse to round a barrel without knocking it over. Should a horse knock over a barrel, precious seconds are added to the rider's time by the judges. The winner is the rider with the fastest time.

Because speed is such an important issue in this short obstacle course, Quarter Horses are used in this event. The horse enters the course at full speed. The movement of the rider and horse past an electronic eye triggers the clock to start timing the run.

Winning ten straight world championships with rider Charmayne James aboard, Gillis Bay Boy, known as "Scamper," is considered the event's most celebrated champion: he was inducted into the Pro Rodeo Hall of Fame in 1995.

Cutting

In a cutting contest a horse and its rider must separate steers from a herd; one by one, within a specified amount of time, usually about two and a half minutes.

A rider singles out a steer for his horse to separate from the herd, then it is up to the horse to show off its skills. The horse must show its dominance over the steer and keep it from rejoining the group. After cutting a steer the horse heads back to the herd to single out another steer. Care must be taken not to disperse the rest of the herd each time the horse returns to select the next steer to separate from the group.

Acrobatic Riding

Mounted on beautiful Arabian horses, European performers have long graced the sport of acrobatic riding. To this day, Ringling Brothers Barnum and Bailey Circus still features three separate elaborately costumed family troupes on horseback, performing simultaneously in each of the circus's famous three rings.

Whether in the rodeo arena or under the big top tent, precision timing is the key to this event. Riders do not sit upon saddles, but perch precariously, standing on the backs of one or more horses. Riders must balance atop moving mounts, sometimes with other performers on their shoulders. Performers will sometimes ride head down between two moving horses.

A cutting horse is trained to separate a cow from its herd. To do so the horse must anticipate the movement of the cow, stay with it as it runs, and prevent it from returning to the herd.

Acrobatic riding has been a proven crowd pleaser since the days of Buffalo Bill Cody's Wild West Shows.

Steer Wrestling

In a steer wrestling contest, a rider and his horse ride to catch up to a steer. Once the horse is alongside the steer, the rider jumps off and grabs hold of the steer's head and horns. Because the steer is still running, a competitor will dig his heels into the ground to slow down the steer. The contestant then attempts to wrestle the animal to the ground. Rules stipulate that the steer must be lying on its side to stop the clock, and the contestant with the fastest time wins.

There once was a cowboy by the name of Bill

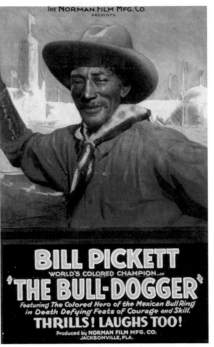

THE NORMAN FILM MFG. CO. PRESENTS

BILL PICKETT
WORLD'S COLORED CHAMPION...
'THE BULL-DOGGER'
Featuring The Colored Hero of the Mexican Bull Ring in Death Defying Feats of Courage and Skill.
THRILLS! LAUGHS TOO!
Produced by NORMAN FILM MFG. CO.
JACKSONVILLE, FLA.

Bill Pickett, the most famous black rodeo star of all time, played himself in the 1922 film The Bulldogger. In 1993 the U.S. Postal Service included Pickett in its "Legends of the West" stamp series, but accidentally used a photo of his brother Ben. 250 million stamps had to be recalled and replaced with the correct photo.

Pickett who became legendary for his unique method of steer wrestling, or bulldogging, as the sport is also called. As a young boy, Pickett had once seen a bulldog bite the lower lip of a cow. He was fascinated by the fact that a small dog could immobilize a large cow. Several days later, on his way to school, he decided to try that same technique himself. By fearlessly biting the lower lip of a calf, he helped incredulous men from the Littlefield Cattle Company to brand an unwieldy animal.

At the age of 15, Pickett began working as a cowhand on ranches all over Texas. He learned how to ride and use a lariat, and he practiced his unique brand of bulldogging every chance he got. Before long, people started spreading the word about the talented cowboy that would bite the lip of a steer. When the Williamson Country Livestock Association brought a fair to Taylor, Texas, Pickett entered the rodeo competition. His trademark bite helped him win a job with the rodeo.

Pickett would use that technique again and again in front of cheering crowds at rodeos and in Wild West shows across the country. After he became an accomplished rodeo star, he and his show horse, Bradley, performed in Mexico, Canada, South America, and before the King and Queen of England in 1914.

In 1971, some 39 years after his death, Bill Pickett was inducted into the National Cowboy Hall of Fame. The son of freed slaves, Pickett was the first African American to earn entry to the Hall.

Rodeos are usually held throughout the western United States. However, the legendary Calgary Stampede is actually held north of the border in neighboring Canada. Tickets for the annual event are sold nearly one year in advance. The event drew 1,218,851 fans in July 2000, setting a new attendance record.

Reining competitions
highlight the skills of a
good cow horse, such as
the ability to switch from a
run to a sudden sliding stop.
To perform the sliding stop,
a horse locks its hindlegs
under itself and slides
forward on its hind feet.

REINING COMPETITION

The National Reining Horse Association (NRHA) was founded in 1966. The governing body of the sport of reining, the NRHA is dedicated to the promotion of the reining horse and sets the standards for the sport. Their motto is: "To rein a horse is not only to guide him, but to control his every movement."

There are many contests designed to showcase a horse's reining skills. To enter such a competition, a horse must be a working type horse, be in good health, and stand over 14.1 hands high. While a person's height is measured in feet, a horse's height is measured in hands. According to U.S. Customary and Imperial British Standards, one hand is equal to

For reining horses to perform at their best, a special footing of loose clay, sand, and silt is used in the show ring.

four inches, or 10.16 centimeters. A reining horse can be of any breed or cross-breed.

At the judge's command, the horses are required to perform on both reins around a ring. Each horse must demonstrate its ability to walk, trot, and canter around the ring. Then the horse and its rider work together to perform various maneuvers that mimic many of the skills required of a good cow horse performing its ranch work.

According to the NRHA, "Reining is a judged event designed to show the athletic ability of a ranch type horse within the confines of a show area. In NRHA competition, contestants are required to run one of ten approved patterns. Each pattern includes small slow circles, large fast circles, flying lead changes, roll backs over the hocks, 360 degree spins done in place, and exciting sliding stops that are the hallmark of the reining horse."

It is no coincidence that cutting horses need to be able to perform roll-backs, flying changes, pivots, and spins while they are working cattle. Many reining of the maneuvers are based on ranch work. While small slow circles and large fast circles are fairly self-explanatory, some of the other maneuvers require some explanation.

Mary Gordon-Watson describes the flying change in great detail in her book, *The Handbook of Riding*. She explains, "In the flying change the horse changes leading legs simultaneously during the moment of suspension which follows the third beat of the canter. He must spring from one pair of leading legs to the other in one movement. Correctly performed, the flying change is the smoothest way of changing direction at the canter (or at the gallop), but it is an advanced movement in that the rider must give exact aids, with split-second timing, fractionally before the moment of suspension." While performing a flying change, the horse must not break from its gait.

The sliding stop, an essential move in calf-roping, is an advanced move for a horse. It requires a horse to stop suddenly by sliding its hind legs under its body. This puts a great deal of strain on the hindquarters of a horse and must be done with extreme care. When a horse is learning to perform the sliding stop, it is usually outfitted with skid boots to help prevent injury. The natural progression is to teach a horse the sliding stop first at a walk, then at a jog, next at a lope, and finally, at a gallop.

For a roll back, a horse must gallop on the left lead before stopping and turning at the same time to the right. It then must continue to gallop forward on the right lead. Horses are usually trained to perform this maneuver after mastering reining back in a small circle.

When a horse reins back, it walks backward in a special way: instead of each leg raising and lowering independently, a horse must raise two legs together. For example, a horse would raise its left front and right rear legs at the same time. This must all be done to a steady two-time beat.

When performing a 360-degree spin, the horse's hind feet serve as the pivot of the circle, with the radius of the circle being the length of the horse's body. This maneuver requires a horse to plant its hind feet while swinging its front feet in bounding movements around them.

In reining competitions there can be one or more judges evaluating a horse. Each horse is given an average score of 70 to begin. Judges can then add or subtract up to one and a half points per maneuver, in increments of a half point, as they evaluate the quality of each maneuver. If a horse makes a major deviation from the pattern, it can be given a zero for that particular go. A horse that makes a minor deviation from the pattern may have points deducted as well.

Previously, judges simply assessed each rider's overall run in the sport of reining, but in 1985 they amended the judging process and now score each maneuver on an individual basis.

Judges give horses credit for attitude, authority, finesse, quickness, and smoothness during the performance of a particular maneuver. The level of difficulty is raised when the horse is required to perform at a controlled speed, so judges award more points accordingly.

In 1990, there were just 3,850 horses registered with the National Reining Horse Association. By the year 2000, with

The Western Saddle

The high pommel, or horn, on the Western saddle not only allowed a cowboy to hang on while galloping or taking sharp turns, it also gave him a place to secure his lariat, or rope. A feisty steer pulling with all its might on the rope's other end would then have to contend with the anchor effect produced by the weight of the cowboy, the saddle, and the horse.

the growth of the sport, there were 10,250 horses registered. There were 100 approved shows for the sport in 1988. By 2000, that number had grown to 345, as the sport gained in popularity.

As interest in reining grew, the money awarded to the sport's winners rose from $1.2 million during 1990 to a whopping $4.5 million paid in NRHA competitions in 2000.

The first sire to win over one million dollars in offspring earnings was Hollywood Jac 86, who realized this milestone in 1993. Since then, Be Aech Enterprise, Hollywood Dun It, Topsail Cody, and Smart Chic Olena have joined this elite club of sires whose offspring have collected over $1,000,000 in prize money.

Fittingly, Hollywood Dun It, who was sired by Hollywood Jac 86, the sport's first million dollar winner, became the sport's first two million dollar sire in the year 2000.

In 1995, leading rider, Bill Horn, one of the founders of the sport of reining, was the first to accumulate over $1 million in winnings from NHRA competitions. He was followed in 1997 by rider Tom McQuay.

In 1998 reining was accepted as the first Western discipline of the United States Equestrian Team, which hopes to make reining an Olympic event.Reining was accepted as an international sport by the Federation Equestre International (FEI) in 2000.

Eyesa Special wins by two lengths to take the 2000 All-American Quarter Horse Futurity—the richest Quarter Horse race in the world—in Ruidoso Downs, New Mexico.

QUARTER HORSE RACING

H orse racing dates back to ancient times. Initially, the horses that were racing had no riders. The horses' owners prepared for a race by simply allowing the horses to become thirsty, and then releasing them at equal distances from a watering hole. The winner was the first to reach the water and drink. In the 7th century the Greeks were the first to put riders atop their race-horses. In those early races, the riders rode bareback. With no saddle to grab, and no toehold or stirrup to help give them a leg up, riders had to be quite fit just to get up onto their horses. The rider had to grip the horse tightly between his thighs, sometimes hanging on to the horse's mane for stability.

The early American colonists worked hard just to exist in their new country, and when the day's work was done, they put an equal amount of effort into their leisure pursuits. Horse racing quickly became popular with many of the colonists. For others, horse racing was soon to became a passion.

In those days, there were no race tracks. The colonists and their horses made do with make-shift racing venues. Horses might race down the main street of the local village, or gallop across a meadow or pasture to a finish line agreed upon by a handshake between business associates.

Just because a race took place on a country lane instead of being run on a real racetrack did not mean that the horse owners were any less passionate about the race's results. Heavy betting on horse races was quite common during colonial times. Sometimes the stakes were very high. A deed to a plantation might be wagered and lost, making someone a homeless loser and someone else a landowner.

With so much at stake, the colonists put a great deal of thought into choosing a horse. They knew that for a horse to be a winner, it must have a steady gait. Each of the horse's four legs must share equally in the scientific business of running. Each leg must touch down an equal amount of times, at even intervals, bearing an equal amount of the horse's weight, to keep a natural rhythm going.

With these facts in mind, the settlers sought to find a horse that would have an advantage on the racetrack. They wanted a horse with speed. In the early 1600s horses that were brought to the colonies by the Spanish were bred with horses brought over by the English and the Irish. The resulting horses were compact, with very powerful leg muscles. This physical combination allowed the new type of horse to get off to an explosive start in a race. The

The American Quarter Horse is known for being quick on its feet. Quarter Horses have a fast, powerful take-off and a sprinting ability that makes them ideal barrel racers.

horse's speed gradually diminished at increasingly longer distances, but for a quarter of a mile, no horse could run faster. It would be named the American Quarter Horse.

The colonists were pleased with this new type of horse, and set about breeding more. The horse that became known as the American Quarter Horse has the distinction of being the first breed of horse native to the United States.

In 1674 Enrico County, Virginia, hosted the first American Quarter Horse races. Since then, dozens of racetracks have become associated with Quarter Horse racing.

Belmont Park, Churchill Downs, and Gulfstream Park are but three of the more famous tracks which typically host Quarter Horse racing.

In 1940 a registry was established to preserve the lineage of the breed. Today a registered American Quarter Horse must have both a numbered American Quarter Horse sire and dam. There is, however, a special appendix to the American Quarter Horse registry which allows a foal to have one of its parents be a numbered American Quarter Horse, and the other be a Thoroughbred registered with the Jockey Club.

Because of these exacting specifications regarding bloodlines, the resulting horses can be one of only 13 accepted colors. No American Quarter Horses are white. Typically, the horse is sorrel, a reddish brown color, but it may also be bay (a brown color with a black mane and tail), black, brown, buckskin, chestnut (a brownish-red color), dun (a grayish yellow), red dun, gray, palomino, red roan (reddish coat with white hairs), blue roan (white coat with

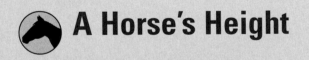 **A Horse's Height**

A horse's height is measured not at the top of the head as a person's is, but at the withers. The withers is the highest point of the back, where the neck meets the back. Height is not measured at a horse's head because getting a horse to hold its head as high as it can is difficult, but the withers is always in the same position. Height is measured in "hands," with each hand equalling four inches. The breeds range in height from more than 18 hands (over six feet at the withers) to less than 6 hands (shorter than two feet at the withers).

black hairs), or grullo (smoky or mouse-colored). The American Quarter Horse may have limited white facial markings. It is also acceptable for the horse to have limited white marking below its knees.

The American Quarter Horse, Refrigerator, is the only member of the breed to have exceeded $2 million in race winnings. Over six years, he won 22 of the 36 races he entered. Dash for Cash holds the distinction of being the greatest sire of American Quarter Horse racehorses. His 1,353 offspring have earned over $37 million. Dash for Cash didn't do badly himself, winning 21 of the 25 races he started.

An American Quarter Horse may well become famous for its speed, or for the speediness of those horses it sires, but some of the breed's well-known names have achieved greatness in other ways as well. For example, many of actor Robert Redford's most beloved co-stars have been American Quarter Horses. A total of 17 of the breed were used in his film, *The Horse Whisperer*. Rambo Roman, known to American movie-goers as Rimrock, is actually owned by Buck Brannaman, who was the inspiration for Redford's film character in *The Horse Whisperer*, Tom Booker. Pilgrim, the leading horse in *The Horse Whisperer*, was played by an unregistered Quarter Horse named Hightower.

Another horse that has appeared in a major film is buck-skin-colored Plain Justin Bar. The film *Dances with Wolves* won the actor/director Kevin Costner the 1991 Academy Award for Best Picture, and Plain Justin Bar was awarded the first American Quarter Horse Silver Spur Award for his outstanding performance as Cisco.

Since then, the prestigious Silver Spur Award has gone to ten-time barrel racing rodeo champion Scamper, as well

"The American Quarter Horse," a painting by Orren Mixer, shows the conformation of the ideal American Quarter Horse.

as Docs Keeping Time. Docs Keeping Time starred in the Warner Brothers movie, *Black Beauty* (based on the novel by Anna Sewall), and has also been featured in a television commercial and a music video. Unsuccessful on the Quarter Horse race track circuit, Docs Keeping Time was very successful as the star of the television series, *The Black Stallion*. He also worked alongside Rambo Roman and Hightower, playing the role of Gulliver, in *The Horse Whisperer*.

Besides racing, today's American Quarter Horse is used for pleasure riding, ranch work, and rodeo riding, particularly for barrel racing and roping events.

In 1956 television actors Clayton Moore and Jay Silverheels appeared in the feature film, *The Lone Ranger*.

RADIO, TELEVISION, AND FILM

The Western horse came into the homes and hearts of Americans through radio, television, and movies. Tom Mix, Roy Rogers, Hopalong Cassidy, Gene Autry, and John Wayne helped to form our idea of the Wild West. People the world over came to think of Americans as cowboys because of the Western theme so prominent in our exported films, radio, and television programs. It's no wonder that people the world over became familiar with American Western movie stereotypes and themes: good guys wear white hats; bad guys wear black; and that it was cowardly to shoot a man in the back. Cowboys lived and died by their own code of ethics, and the media's version of cowboys faithfully promoted these moral mandates to their fans.

Tom Mix was a silent film star who would go on to radio fame. In real life, Thomas Hezekiah Mix was born in 1880 and died in 1940. His larger-than-life radio character, however, would live on until June 1950, when television spelled doomed for radio's once popular programs. Throughout the program's lengthy run, several actors lent their voices to portray the character of Cowboy Marshal Tom Mix.

Making its debut in September 1933, *The Tom Mix Radio Show* was sponsored by Ralston Cereal. The radio show was a big hit with kids, and the cereal company's sales soared. For almost 20 years, premiums were offered to the program's listeners. Fans could receive anything from bandannas to branding irons to badges, and nearly everything in between by sending in cereal box tops.

Tom Mix, his horse Tony, and his Straight Shooters fought crime from the TM Bar Ranch near Dobie, Texas, on the radio series. The premiums that were awarded by Ralston Cereal to loyal listeners who sent in their box tops are still traded today by fans who have hung onto their Mix memorabilia.

Gene Autry was such a popular recording artist, movie and radio star, and rodeo performer that in 1941, the town of Berwyn, Oklahoma, was renamed Gene Autry, Oklahoma. Known as "the Singing Cowboy," Autry was showered with honors, including being inducted to the Country Music, Nashville Songwriters, and the National Cowboy Halls of Fame.

Billed as "The King of Cowboys," Roy Rogers brought the code of the West and the American cowboy to thousands of TV viewers around the world. The smiling Rogers and his faithful horse, Trigger, were welcomed into the

Born in 1880, silent film star Tom Mix, shown with Tony "the Wonder Horse," appeared in over 300 westerns, and by the early 1920s, his fame earned him $10,000 a week. Mix made his last movie in 1935, but his legend lived on through broadcasts of the much-loved *Tom Mix Radio Show.*

homes of families during the 1930s, and remained household names for decades to come. The cowboy and his horse graced the cover of *Life* in 1943, and by 1950 there were 2000 Roy Rogers fan clubs around the world. London's club, the world's largest, boasted over 50,000 members.

Roy's real-life wife, Dale Evans, co-starred on his long running television series, and harmonized with her husband on the show's closing theme song, "Happy Trails to You."

Roy Rogers died on July 6, 1998, but many members of his Roy Rogers Riders Club still have, somewhere in their possession, the membership card that they were issued when they first joined, containing these ten rules to live by:

1. Be neat and clean.
2. Be courteous and polite.
3. Always obey your parents.
4. Protect the weak and help them.
5. Be brave, but never take chances.
6. Study hard and learn all you can.
7. Be kind to animals and care for them.
8. Eat all your food and never waste any.
9. Love God and go to Sunday school regularly.
10. Always respect our flag and our country.

Roy Rogers would be known to younger generations as the namesake behind a fast food franchise that specialized in fried chicken and roast beef sandwiches, but to their

 **Trigger**

Golden Cloud was a Palomino born in 1932. He later became known as Trigger when he rode down many happy trails with his on-screen partner and owner, Roy Rogers.

Trigger's saddle was encrusted with 1,000 glittering red rubies and cost $50,000.

Before retiring in 1957, the four-legged movie star, known as "The Smartest Horse in the Movies," starred in 87 films and 101 television shows.

Trigger had been such a constant in Rogers's life that the cowboy couldn't bear to bury the horse when it died in 1965. Instead, Rogers had Trigger mounted by a taxidermist and put on display in his museum.

grandparents, he was an idol who cheered them up during America's Great Depression and helped teach them right from wrong.

Starting as a radio show and winding up as a popular television series, *The Lone Ranger* was another program that helped deliver the cowboy's code of ethics to several generations of American youngsters. Clayton Moore played "the Masked Man" on television, beginning in September 1949. Each program began with a rousing rendition of the William Tell Overture, and the dramatic words, "The Lone Ranger! 'Hi, Yo, Silver!'"

Like Roy Rogers, the Lone Ranger had a creed by which he lived. Fran Striker, the show's original writer, wrote the cowboy's creed, which included, "I believe that to have a friend, a man must be one," and "I believe in being prepared physically, mentally, and morally to fight when necessary for that which is right."

Native American Jay Silverheels played the Lone Ranger's faithful Indian companion, Tonto, making it clear that as far as the Lone Ranger was concerned, the long standing feud between the nation's cowboys and Indians was over. Together, Tonto and the Lone Ranger fought the good fight for law and order in America's new frontier, both in the television series, and in the 1956 feature length film, *The Lone Ranger.*

Silver, the Masked Man's trusted white steed, was a beautiful specimen of a horse, and like the ever-present white hat on the Lone Ranger's head, he served as a symbol for all that was good and pure.

Much loved in the movies and throughout American history, the Western horse continues to thrive in the United States today as a work, pleasure, sport, and performance horse.

1492	Columbus brings horses to the Americas
1519	The explorer Cortez brings horses to Mexico
1539	Explorer Hernando De Soto brings 237 horses to North America
1609–11	25 horses are imported to Virginia from England
1665	Hempstead Plains on Long Island, New York, becomes the first established race course in North America
1674	Enrico County, Virginia hosts the first American Quarter Horse races
1730's	England sends Thoroughbreds to the southern colonies
1860	The Pony Express carries mail from St. Joseph, Missouri, to San Francisco in the record time of ten days
1877	The tribal lands of the Nez Perce are seized by United States; the Appaloosa and its breeders are nearly wiped out.
1887	Buffalo Bill Cody's Wild West Show performs before Queen Victoria in England
1938	The Appaloosa Horse Club is formed and the breed is revived
1940	A stud book is established for the American Quarter Horse
1949	*The Lone Ranger* makes its television debut
1971	Bill Pickett becomes the first African American named to the Cowboy Hall of Fame
1993	Refrigerator becomes the first American Quarter Horse to top $2 million in racing prizes
1997	Jeff Chapman of Athens, Texas, ropes a calf in a record 6.8 seconds at the National Finals Rodeo
2000	A Ransom, an American Quarter Horse with bloodlines tracing to the legendary Dash for Cash, is named World Champion

GLOSSARY

Appaloosa—breed of horse with a spotted coat

Bareback—riding a horse without a saddle

Breed—a group of horses descended from a common ancestor, that share certain physical traits and characteristics

Buck—when a horse bucks, it kicks out with its strong, rear legs; riders are often thrown from a horse when it bucks.

Chaps—leather bibs worn over a Western rider's pants to protect the legs from brush while riding

Coat—a horse's fur or hair is referred to as its coat

Corral—an area where horses are kept fenced in

Cue—a signal that a rider gives the horse, asking it to perform a specific action; reins, legs, feet, and voice commands can all be used to cue a horse

Fetlock—a hair-covered bump on the horse's leg, just above the hoof

Foal—name for a baby horse

Forelock—part of a horse's mane that grows forward between its ears and onto its face.

Gait—the pace at which a horse moves

Groom—to brush and clean a horse

Halter—a piece of rope, leather, or nylon that a horse wears on its head

Jog—a gait that falls between a walk and a lope; English riders use the term trot for the jog gait

Lariat—a leather or horsehair rope designed for throwing and lassoing

Lasso—another word for lariat; it is also the word used to mean throwing a rope around something for the purpose of pulling it in

Lope—a gait that is faster than a jog but slower than a gallop

Paint—a type of horse with different colors in its coat

Palomino—a golden horse with a white mane and tail

Pinto—a type of horse whose coat has irregular splotches of color

Quarter Horse—American breed of horse best known for its ability to run well for one quarter of a mile, also popular with pleasure riders and ranchers

Rodeo—an event in which riders compete in such sports as calf roping or saddle bronc riding

Rope—to throw a rope around an animal's neck

Saddlebag—a bag that hangs from the saddle and is used to carry supplies

Spurs—spiked metal items attached to a rider's boots

Tack—horse equipment including a bridle, saddle, saddle pad, and blanket

GaWaNi Pony Boy. *Out of the Saddle: Native American Horsemanship.* Irvine, California: Bow Tie Press, 1998.

Gordon-Watson, Mary. *The Handbook of Riding.* New York: Alfred A. Knopf, 1986.

McCall, Edith. *Frontiers of America: Mail Riders, Paul Revere to Pony Express.* New York: Children's Press, Inc., 1961.

Morris, Desmond. *Horsewatching.* New York: Crown Publishers, Inc., 1988.

Parelli, Pat, and Katy Kadash. *Natural Horse-Man-Ship.* Colorado Springs, Colorado: Western Horseman, Inc., 1993.

Pinkney Andrea, and Brian Pinkey, illustrator. *Bill Pickett Rodeo-Ridin' Cowboy.* New York: Harcourt Brace & Company, 1996.

Ward, Lesley. *The Horse Illustrated Guide to Western Riding.* Irvine, California: Bowtie Press, 1998.

page:
2:	David F. Clobes
6:	Library of Congress
11:	Library of Congress
13:	Library of Congress
14:	Photo by Don Shugart—Compliments of the Appaloosa Horse Club
17:	John Macken
20:	John Macken
24:	Charles Mann Photography
28:	Galyn Hammond
33:	Bruce Carr/Freedom Photography
35:	Charles Mann Photography

37:	Galyn Hammond
38:	Library of Congress
40:	Charles Mann Photography
42:	Charles Mann Photography
46:	AP/Wide World Photos
49:	Reprinted with permission from the American Quarter Horse Association
52:	Reprinted with permission from the American Quarter Horse Association
54:	Library of Congress
57:	Library of Congress

Front Cover Photo: © Kevin R. Morris/CORBIS

MARY HUGHES graduated from the University of Maryland with a degree in Radio, Television, and Film. She enjoyed substitute teaching for many years before tackling her current assignment as a computer lab tech at an elementary school in Maryland. Her first book, a biography of comedian Jim Carrey, written for Chelsea House's "Overcoming Adversity Series," was named to the New York Public Library's list of "Best Books for the Teen Age" in 1999. An avid baseball fan, Ms. Hughes writes feature articles about ballplayers in the Baltimore Orioles organization. Writing as she does about both the minor and major leaguers, she often gets an inside peek at just what it takes to make it to the big leagues, and how special it can be to remain there.